art | commerce

art | commerce

four artisan businesses grow in an old New Jersey industrial city

text and photographs by

Steven J. Riskind

introductory essay by

Philip Scranton

art | commerce

four artisan businesses grow in an old New Jersey industrial city

ISBN 978-0-578-68425-3

Library of Congress Control Number: 2020907536

Publisher
steve riskind photography
Steven J. Riskind
Ridgewood, NJ

Contents

Artisanship in Paterson: A Tradition of Specialty Work

Philip Scranton

University Board of Governors Professor of History Emeritus, Rutgers University

It's truly a pleasure to have the opportunity to introduce Steve Riskind's profiles of current-day Paterson artisans. As will soon be apparent to you, this volume is both a visual treat and an information banquet, for it introduces a cluster of remarkable people doing extraordinary work in a city whose industrial prominence faded generations ago. My job is to frame that historical context briefly, sketching Paterson's long trajectory as a center for just the sort of skill- and quality-intensive production displayed in the following pages.

In the chronicle of American history, Paterson usually appears only twice. The city first sprouted near a site where, in the 1790s, Alexander Hamilton (yes, that Alexander Hamilton) and associates began harnessing the Passaic River's Great Falls to power their Society for Establishing Useful Manufactures' yarn spinning and cotton printing ventures. Sadly, their heralded industrial experiment lasted just three years, closing in 1797, a victim of skilled labor shortages, insufficient technical knowledge and the personal bankruptcies of several directors. Second, over a century later, Paterson again burst onto the national scene as the anchor-point for a massive labor conflict: the 1913 silk strike, led by the much-feared Industrial Workers of the World, a revolutionary union that welcomed women and immigrants to its ranks (unusual at the time). Proximity to New York City, whose fashion trades had spurred expansion of Paterson's fine and fancy silk weaving, guaranteed widespread press coverage of the dramatic conflict. For months, family firm owners and partners, many having relocated from Britain and northern Europe, faced off against thousands of spinners, weavers, and dyers, mostly recent arrivals from Southern Europe, especially Italy. After months, the mill owners did prevail; but later observers credited the strikers' resilience as reinforcing manufacturers' already-evident trend to build new plants in the coal and steel counties of northeastern Pennsylvania, where thousands of "idle" wives could be recruited for textile work. Paterson's long slow decline had begun.

Nonetheless, nineteenth century Paterson had grounded its

reputation on craftsmanship and skill, developing what is sometimes called "specialty production," the capacity to make quality goods, individually customized or in batches, in many varieties to meet precise and varying demands. This is, essentially, the opposite of mass production – making thousands or millions of identical items, whether simple goods like paper clips or complicated ones like Ford's Model T's. Thus in metalworking, Paterson firms fabricated machinery and built steam locomotives, rather than making nails and rails by the ton. In textiles, early firms made spools of tough "sewing silks and cottons" in scores of colors for home or workshop use with the steadily- proliferating Singer sewing machines. Many enterprises at first threw (silk spinning is called 'throwing') coarse, then soon, finer yarns for looms running ribbons, velvets and other fashion fabrics, dyed or printed locally to match seasonal trends. Moving up the skills ladder, they gradually mastered the intricacies of designing and weaving Jacquard goods in extravagant Second Empire patterns combining a dozen or more colors. Accumulating both technical and design skills, Paterson secured an international reputation as "Silk City," becoming a magnet which drew immigrant workers fleeing Italy's depressed late nineteenth century economy, a portion of whom had silk industry experience. (Italy and France then led European silk production, but the French rarely emigrated.)

Moreover, resonating with the enterprises reviewed below, Paterson became a hothouse for artisan entrepreneurship, beginning roughly in the 1850s. Not only did the city's specialty firms attract ambitious skilled workers hoping to start their own operations, area real estate investors created the necessary spaces for launching their small startups. At a time when giant New England textile corporations erected blocks-long plants for their exclusive use at Lowell or Lawrence, MA, Paterson builders constructed mid-size brick factories offering "rooms with power" to multiple tenants. The owners installed and maintained a central steam engine which delivered motive power to machines through overhead (or subfloor) shafts, gears and belts. Tenants rented sections of factory floors (so much a square foot), which lessors sectioned off with panels or screens, and routinely either bought or leased looms that their predecessors left behind when departing (whether to seek jobs after failing or larger quarters when successful). This innovative support for entrepreneurs, duplicated in Providence, Philadelphia and elsewhere, dramatically lowered initial costs. Instead of needing, say, $20,000 (ca. 1890) to construct or buy a building, purchase machinery and accessories, then manage fixed operating costs while creating designs, hiring/ training workers and seeking agents to market finished goods, a skilled Paterson silk weaver (or machinist for that matter) with only a few hundred dollars could handle the carrying costs of a room-with-power lease, rent a few used looms, and hire family members or *paesani* from Old Country home towns to turn out product samples. To be sure, the failure rate was phenomenal. Business directories of Paterson textile firms, used by materials and supplies sellers and by marketing agents seeking goods for resale, documented hundreds of local companies annually. In hard times, a third of one year's operators disappeared from the next year's listings, replaced by scores of newcomers trying to turn unemployment into self- employment. Academic studies suggest that 80% of such tiny startups closed within five years, not least because their thin capital resources could not withstand the economy's recurrent recessions and depressions. (Before the 2020 smash, by comparison, about 55% of US startups in the 2010-19 decade failed within five years, a better outcome perhaps, but still tough on entrepreneurs.)

Before the Great Depression, Paterson industries faced hard times across the board. Metalworking had begun fading away in the 1910s; the Rogers locomotive factory closed in the year of the great silk strike, becoming a spare parts workshop and storage unit. Silk goods provided minimal profits in the 1920s as wholesalers and department store purchasing consolidating, giving buyers market power to drive prices lower. Worse, the first synthetic fabric, rayon, took off in women's wear – cheaper than silk and less durable, it symbolized the advent of throwaway fashion. The Second World

War ended imports of Chinese and Japanese raw silk, but many city factories already rested vacant. Some mills were demolished, but other spaces, as the following chapters amply demonstrate, remained vital or eventually welcomed new tenants whose artisan talents richly echo those of dimly-remembered predecessors. Now that Steve Riskind has opened those workshop doors, to enter the enduring world of Paterson creativity just turn the page.

[Now emeritus professor of history at Rutgers, Phil Scranton has long researched the textile industry in the Mid-Atlantic, ca. 1800-1950, and specialty manufacturing nationally during the 20th century. An early product of these projects was an essay collection he edited – Silk City: Studies of the Paterson Silk Industry, 1860-1940, Newark: New Jersey Historical Society, 1985 – which interested readers might consult for further information.]

Photographer's Introduction

Steve Riskind

The photographs in this book are a fusion of two passions in my life as a photographer: the industrial landscape and portraiture.

The Industrial Landscape

I first learned photography from Robert Donald Erickson, my high school art teacher at the University of Chicago's Lab School. Bob Erickson was a Renaissance man: a visual artist, a toy design consultant, a trained musician, and a photographer. He built his own cameras, some of which we were able to use in class.

Bob Erickson purchased a large stash of WW II surplus film with which we were encouraged to experiment. His dictum to students was that we were welcome to use as much of the film for projects as we wanted, but we could not waste it. I remember making a short film in which the camera (not really, it only looked that way) was flushed down a toilet with Bach's D Minor Toccata and Fugue for organ playing in the background. Erickson enjoyed it immensely.

But not all was play and experiment. I learned about the Minor White and Ansel Adams Zone System, a framework and technique for achieving control over the dynamic range of black and white photographs. At the end of four years, besides breathing lots of Dektol developer fumes in the darkroom, I had a strong knowledge of the foundations of photography. And I'd had a great deal of fun.

Bob Erickson was a wonderful teacher. He was also a rational and caring human being who in many ways served as a surrogate father for me. My own father, having dealt with years of my mother's illness and eventual death, had difficulty accepting and supporting an unconventional son.

Erickson's own photography documented landscape and people in a gritty industrial city. Some years ago, I was given a catalog of Erickson's photographs by the Stephen Dater Gallery in Chicago, which had presented an exhibition of Erickson's work, "The Lens of the Total Designer." Bob Erickson did not usually show us his own work in class, but in looking through this catalog, I was struck by how similar my own style was to his.

I continued taking and developing photographs through college, graduate school, and into the 1970s. My enlarger, safelight, timer, and trays are still in the basement. As my computer consulting business began to take more and more of my time and energy, my photography was set aside.

Around 2010, I began to scale back the software development work. At loose ends, my wife suggested that I might consider taking photography courses. I explored the offerings at the International Center of Photography (ICP) in New York City. Bernd Nobel, a faculty member, suggested that I re-learn my photographic skills in the digital realm. After years of computer consulting, I had all the computing resources and knowledge I needed to immerse myself in digital photography. ICP classes were hands-on, and I had many opportunities to take photographs in the New York City area. I particularly remember trips to the Gowanus Canal in Brooklyn as part of Victoria Rich's class "The Hidden Landscape of the City."

I have been asked why I find so much appeal in photographing old and often crumbling urban landscapes. Undoubtedly, some of the appeal came from growing up in Chicago. Early in the morning you could hear the far-away roar of the mills along the lakefront in South Chicago and Gary, Indiana. Chicago was filled with bridges and other steel structures. My eyes were drawn to these as were Bob Erickson's before me. At the Lab School, housed in 19th century university buildings, I had the chance to tinker with old physics and electronic equipment. One of my high school jobs was to run closed-circuit TV cables through the University's steam tunnels. I am right at home in places filled with spare parts. You will see this love in some of the photographs in this book.

Work around the Gowanus Canal led to my series of photographs of an abandoned limestone processing plant in Cheshire, Massachusetts. The place was huge, empty, and creepy. There were signs of human habitation, possibly homeless people living there. I never knew what to expect when I slipped in. In fact, no one threatened me in the mill, and I made many trips there to take photographs. The Cheshire Mill photographs were the basis of a solo exhibition in 2010.

Following the work at Cheshire, I began to explore industrial landscapes closer to home. A neighbor, who grew up in Paterson, less than a half-hour drive from where we live, took me to the American Textile Printing site. Fenced in, though you could easily sneak through, near the Paterson Great Falls, the ATP site contained a number of abandoned factory buildings and a variety of urban landscape photography opportunities.

Over a period of several years, I made many trips to the ATP site. I also began exploring other areas in Paterson. The downtown area, almost completely rebuilt after the great fire of 1902, has a number of beautiful office buildings. At ground floor level, there are now cell phone stores, banks, and a variety of shops. The upper floors are largely vacant. While there were many beautiful architectural details and streetscapes, many of my photographs dealt with decay and abandonment.

My final urban landscape project in Paterson involved the Hinchliffe Brewery. Little remains of the original brewery that closed during Prohibition. The two red brick buildings still standing are a fraction of the original complex, and these buildings were extensively damaged by fire in the 1990s. The structures are massive, and my goal was to photograph them in great detail by stitching together a large number of images into a single high-resolution digital photograph. The stitching, done in Photoshop, requires that you place the camera on a tripod and take a series of pictures, row by row, until you have photographed the entire subject. Each picture was made up of approximately thirty separate digital images.

This work is time-consuming. It required me to slip through the fence, set up my tripod on a pile of rubble, and carefully reposition the camera after each shot. I photographed the building from a number of angles, and the slow, careful nature of the work left me feeling vulnerable. I was glad to get out alive. Learning, shortly after completing the series of pictures, that someone had recently been murdered in the area of the brewery, convinced me that I did not want to continue this kind of work. I began thinking about other ways I might take photographs of the industrial landscape.

Portraiture

My love of portraiture also begins with my high school teacher Bob Erickson. Erickson had built a beautiful 8" x 10" view camera. Made of wood, the front of the box-like camera had a place to mount a large lens, and the rear had a slot into which you could slide a cut film holder. The camera stood on a heavy wooden tripod.

The 8" x 10" sheets of film we used were not very light sensitive, and the camera required an exposure of a few seconds. The procedure for taking a picture involved placing a black baseball cap over the lens, pulling out the slide in front of the sheet of film in the film holder, then doffing the hat, counting "one thousand one, one thousand two, one thousand three," placing the cap back over the lens, and pushing the slide back down over the sheet of film.

There was a young woman in my class, Kathy Bailey, whom I liked (I was in my early-teens). I asked Kathy if she would sit for a portrait. She agreed, and I set up the camera in a garden in back of our school building. I took a few pictures and headed for the darkroom. A miracle: I got the exposure and the focus right; furthermore, Kathy had sat perfectly still while the baseball cap was off the lens. After the film was developed and dried, I made a contact print of the 8" x 10"

negative. Since the negative was so large, there was no need to make an enlargement.

I was excited. I was going to impress my classmate with a gorgeous portrait. I asked Kathy to come down to Mr. Erickson's art room to show her the picture. She took one look, screamed that it was terrible, and ran out. Heartbreak.

With Mr. Erickson's help, I figured out what had happened. The film I had used, common at the time, was orthochromatic. Unlike the panchromatic film that largely replaced it, ortho film is not sensitive to red light. Kathy, and I, as young teens had lots of zits. Red light, reflected from pimples, does not expose the orthochromatic film, so there are clear spots on the negative. When you make a print from the negative, these blemishes look black. You don't want to emphasize skin blemishes in photos of high school students. In the digital world, this is something I can easily fix in Photoshop, but in the 1950s, this was a problem.

I told Kathy this story at a high school reunion a few years ago. She did not remember the incident, but was mortified at what she had done. I assured her that I understood completely, and that this was all part of my learning photography.

After this experience, I was not enthusiastic about taking portraits for many years. At ICP, however, this began to change. In the introduction to digital photography classes, we had a wide variety of assignments, and I had some success experiences photographing people.

I decided to take a portraiture course. Billy (Liam) Cunningham taught a class on taking portraits that looked at the relationship between the photographer and his or her subject. I am a technical person by nature, but this was the least technical class I had ever taken – never a mention of shutter speeds or f-stops. While a very different approach to photography than Bob Erickson's, Billy Cunningham's approach also encouraged experimentation and emotional honesty. I shared with him my story about Kathy Bailey and my leaving portraiture for fifty years.

Billy Cunningham's class led me in three directions. The first was that I continued to study portraiture at ICP. Cunningham and a number of other teachers there had worked and studied with the famous fashion and portrait photographer Richard Avedon. While I never met Avedon, I've had the honor of studying with several people who had worked with him.

The second outcome was that I was encouraged to continue practicing portraiture. For many years my wife and I have attended summer concerts at the Marlboro Chamber Music Festival in southern Vermont. I had spent a number of summers helping them build a database of musical performances at the festival. I asked about the possibility of taking portraits of the musicians who participate. Thus began a project that has lasted for over ten years. In addition to loving the music, it is a joy for me, from time-to-time, to see my photographs in the program of a concert we are attending.

The third outcome of Billy's class is that I have come to love photographing people.

My Passions Converge

After the Hinchliffe Brewery project, I began to feel that I would be more comfortable photographing businesses around Paterson – but working on the inside. After some searching, I was introduced to Jerry Valenta who owns a small, specialty textile mill that his father had founded after the Second World War. Jerry Valenta and Sons was, to me, an unusual business. There were no employees. With very few exceptions, the only humans on site were Jerry and his son Rich. They have ten Jacquard looms in a cinder block building located in a town just north of Paterson. Jerry was very welcoming, and for a year I made frequent visits to photograph the industrial landscape

inside of his mill. My initial impression was of machinery that ran with infrequent human intervention. Jerry Valenta gave me free run of his mill, and I became intrigued with the machinery. The result was a series of abstract photographs of the looms and ancillary equipment in a small textile mill. These photographs make up the bulk of the first chapter in this book.

After about a year of photographing, the project was beginning to feel complete. Jerry and I collaborated on an exhibition at the Salon 5 Gallery in Riverdale, New Jersey.

I was now ready to photograph other small businesses. While searching around, the owner of a jewelry-manufacturing firm in Paterson, Jan Palombo, stopped by my booth at a crafts fair where I was selling prints of my Paterson photographs. Jan suggested that I might want to photograph her firm which was located in a converted silk mill on the east side of Paterson. I took her up on the offer. Unlike Valenta and Sons, Great Falls Metalworks, the firm Jan and her husband had started, did have employees. While Jan's husband (deceased well before I met Jan) had built many jigs and tools to aid the process of making jewelry, the work was done by Jan, her daughter, and a small group of skilled employees.

For me, successfully photographing Jan and her employees meant photographing both the people and the industrial environment they worked in. How did they transform their materials, pieces of metal and stones, into jewelry? How could I capture their skill and their intensity as they performed the act of transformation? As I reviewed the pictures from the previous photo shoot and thought about what I would do differently the next time I went to Great Falls, I came back to these questions again and again.

There were so many technical considerations. I did not want to use flash and disturb the artisans' concentration. How could I get enough light through the camera's lens to take a clear picture? I found that I was working fairly close, and I needed to find ways to maintain sufficient depth-of-field, trying to keep both the artisan and what she or he was working on in focus. Sometimes the background helped to tell a story in the picture; sometimes it was a distraction. These often-contradictory goals gnawed at me. I addressed them both in the photo shoot and in post processing, editing on the computer after taking the picture.

As I struggled to make all these things happen, I began to realize that this was both urban landscape and portrait photography. In this one project, my two passions were converging.

At the end of the Great Falls Metalworking project, I began to search for a third firm to photograph. After contacting several firms that were not interested, I was sensing a dead end. Then a long-time interest of mine provided a lead.

I have loved pipe organ music for many years. I took organ lessons for a while, and I subscribe to a publication about pipe organs, The Diapason. The Diapason publishes a resource guide each year, a listing of organ builders and firms and organizations that are resources to organ builders and organists. I was leafing through the resource guide where I saw a listing for the Peragallo Pipe Organ Company in Paterson. I remembered an American Guild of Organists tour in Paterson years ago where we had an opportunity to listen to Peragallo instruments. I sent them a query, and they expressed interest in my project.

The Peragallo family welcomed me, and photographing there was a particular treat because I already knew a great deal about the instruments and how they work. Peragallo Pipe Organ was somewhere in the middle of the continuum between the hand work of Great Falls and the zero employees/ten looms of Valenta and Sons. A great deal of skilled hand work goes into a pipe organ, but Peragallo and Company utilizes technology to complement the

work of artisans. The Peragallos allowed me to take photographs in their shop as well as well as in churches where they installed and maintained pipe organs. A rubber bulb to blow wood chips off the camera and lens became a critical tool when photographing in Peragallo's busy wood shop.

Finding the final firm to photograph in the project was easy. John Peragallo, III suggested I contact the Hiemer Stained Glass Studio. Hiemer Stained Glass is located only a few blocks from the Peragallo shop, and John III knew of them because both firms do the vast majority of their work in churches.

Like Peragallo Pipe Organ Company, Hiemer Stained Glass is a family-owned firm in its fourth generation. Judith Hiemer Van Wie, who owns the firm with her husband, proudly told me that stained glass windows are made today in almost the exact manner as they were in the great cathedrals of Europe. There are computers in the front office, and while they do use electric drills and soldering irons, stained glass is the work of highly trained artisans using ancient techniques. There were times during this project when I thought of presenting the photographs in black and white, an aesthetic I learned to love in Bob Erickson's classes, but color is so right for a stained glass studio!

I had not quite reached the end of my journey. In looking at the photographs from all four artisan businesses, I realized that almost no humans were present in the Valenta and Sons images. My goals to show humans transforming materials and the intensity of skilled people at work crystallized after I had photographed Jerry's business. But, in fact, Jerry and Rich were constantly interacting with their looms – setting up new jobs, trouble shooting when a thread broke, doing all manner of quality control. I asked Jerry if I might return to Valenta and Sons to take pictures of them working with the looms. He agreed, and the photographs in that chapter include the first and the last images taken in this series.

When I left for college, I was a science and electronics geek. I did not know whether I would study physics or electrical engineering. I ultimately studied social and organizational psychology. After working in organization development for a number of years, I switched to running a one person (sometimes two person) computer-consulting firm. Just as my photographic work touched on the gritty Chicago industrial landscape and on portraiture, in my life I have steered a course between human interaction and technology. The fusion of these two long-term interests over the eight years of work that led to this book has been highly satisfying. I continue to photograph artisan businesses, and more recently I have begun to photograph visual artists at work. I hope that through this book I can share my journey with you.

This introduction is being written while sheltering at home during the coronavirus pandemic of 2020. None of the four businesses in this book can be considered "essential" businesses that must stay open during the pandemic. I worry that these artisan businesses will suffer in the same way that the arts will suffer during this economic cataclysm. My hope is that they will survive and continue to grow. As with much of life now, we must wait and see.

Acknowledgments

As the introduction suggests, my work in photography is a testament to the role great teachers can play in one's life. It has been almost 60 years since I studied with Robert Erickson, and yet I still feel his influence. Billy Cunningham (not the Bill Cunningham whose photographs graced the Styles Section of the New York Times for so many years) also made a significant contribution. He helped merge the behavioral scientist in me with the more technical person who wants to know as much as possible about how cameras and lenses work. He gave me the confidence I needed to work closely with portraiture subjects. That rapport with subjects, which you must establish while you are also thinking about camera angles, lighting, backdrops, and radio triggers, is key to taking great portraits.

I am grateful to the support and help from two friends, Doug Goodell and Carol Wolf. Doug, a skilled nature photographer, frequently offered technical assistance and encouragement in photography as well as the process of creating this book. Carol, a fine graphic artist, provided support and guidance in turning these photographs and essays into a coherent book.

My great thanks to Sandra Scarry. Sandra is a friend and the co-author of an English and writing textbook, *The Writer's Workplace*. Her editing skills contributed greatly to the readability of *art | commerce*.

Saul Robbins, on the ICP faculty, has consulted with me on the trajectory of my photography career. He provided invaluable help in selecting and sequencing photographs.

I am deeply indebted to Dr. Philip Scranton, Emeritus Board of Governors Professor, History of Industry & Technology, Rutgers University. When I showed Phil an early version of this book, he offered to write an economic overview. I was honored by his offer. I believe it adds a wonderful balance to what I have put together. The photographs of the businesses focus on the work of individuals, and the essays that introduce each chapter are about individual firms and the people who founded and nurtured them. Phil understands the history of Paterson, New Jersey, and the ways Paterson industry changed over time. His essay sets the stage for the growth of these small artisan businesses in and around Paterson.

One of the joys of this project has been getting to know the owners of the four artisan businesses I photographed. Jerry Valenta was welcoming and extremely helpful as I began photographing his family's textile business. Jerry taught me so much about Jacquard looms and the business of specialty weaving. I am deeply indebted to Jerry for his contribution to this project.

Jan Palombo, who founded Great Falls Metalworks with her husband Michael Brothers, gave me access to their facility for many, many visits. She taught me much about the techniques they used for creating jewelry. In addition to this technical knowledge, I am pleased that Jan was willing to share with me much of the personal history of creating the business.

While I already had an understanding of how a pipe organ works, John Peragallo III and his son John IV taught me so much more about the functioning of a pipe organ and how they run an active business that builds, restores, and maintains pipe organs. Peragallo Pipe Organ Company has the most employees of any of the firms I photographed. Since it is a very active place with many tasks taking place simultaneously, I am very thankful that John III and John IV took time away from their busy schedules to help me pursue this project.

Judith Hiemer Van Wie was my main contact at Hiemer Stained Glass Studio. Judi is the fourth generation of her family in the stained glass business. Judi and her husband James, who own the business welcomed me into their operation. Judi, besides being a trained stained glass journeyman, has a deep knowledge of her family's business, the history of making stained glass, and of Church iconography. This was my first contact with a stained glass business, and she brought me up-to-speed quickly. I was given free rein to talk to and photograph Hiemer's journeymen (the term applies to men and women). As a digital photographer working in color, taking pictures in a stained glass studio is a joy.

Creating this book was more than taking and editing photographs. It was an opportunity to get to know four groups of smart and caring people. I am honored that I was allowed to work with these four businesses, and through this book I hope to share my experiences with my readers.

I would especially like to thank my wife Mary. She has been my partner in a journey of more than fifty years. A retired public library director and the author of three children's books, she is also a fine editor. She has never been afraid to tell me when my text makes no sense. One of the things I appreciate about our relationship is that she can give, and I (usually) can accept, this kind of hard feedback. Ultimately, what I say here is my responsibility, but Mary has made a huge contribution to the clarity of this book and to making it say what I really wanted it to say. Her support is so deeply appreciated.

Ridgewood, New Jersey
May 2020

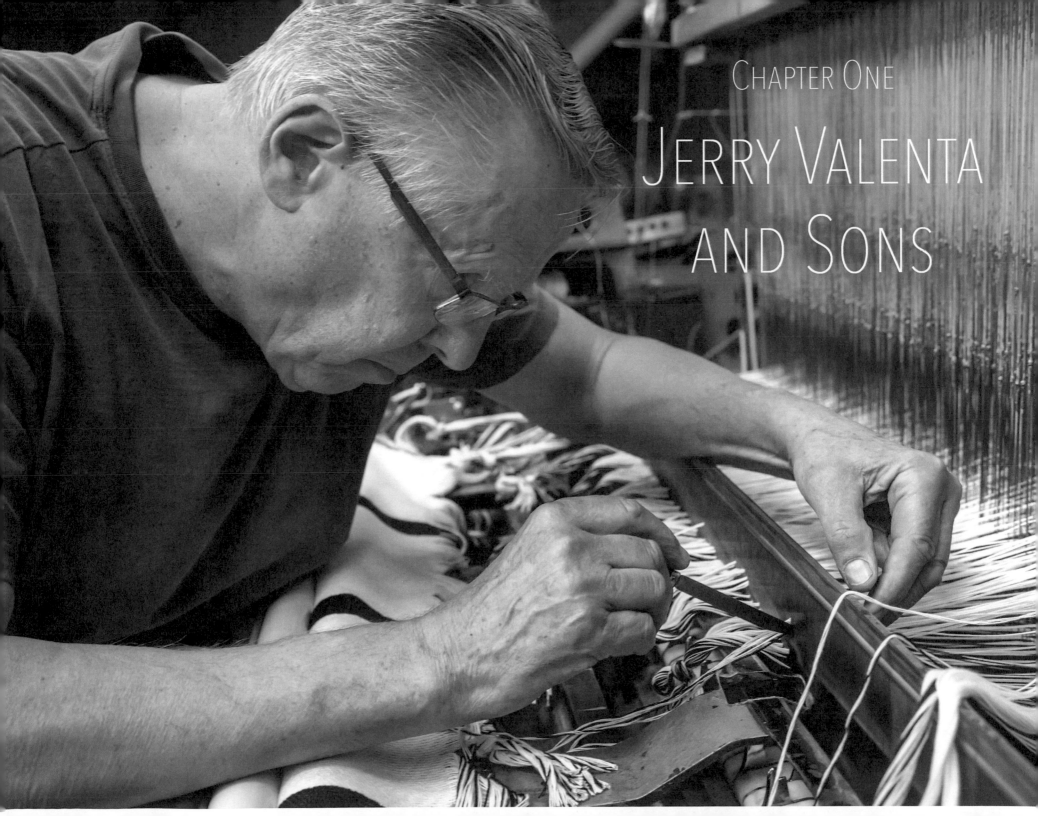

CHAPTER ONE
JERRY VALENTA AND SONS

The founder of Jerry Valenta & Sons, Inc., Jaroslov Valenta, loosely translated as "Jerry," came to the United States in 1929 from Czechoslovakia. The Jerry Valenta I know, one of the sons of Jaroslav Valenta, and with whom I worked on this photo project is named Gerald Valenta, but he, too, goes by the name Jerry. In this essay, I will refer to Jerry's father as Jerry Senior.

In the early 1950s Jerry Senior worked for a Jacquard mill in Waldwick, New Jersey, named Meadox Weaving Company, a maker of drapery and upholstery fabrics. In 1954 Titus Haffa, a Chicago businessman purchased Meadox. Haffa appointed William von Liebig as general manager. [1] Von Liebig brought to the job both experience as a manager and a strong interest in medical science and technology. Titus Haffa's wife had come through a serious vascular operation performed by Dr. Ormond C. Julian. Dr. Julian, along with Michael DeBakey and a number of other physicians, pioneered the use of artificial grafts in vascular surgery. In appreciation for the success of his wife's procedure, Haffa offered to support research at the Meadox Mill to develop artificial veins. William von Liebig, the general manager at the time, and Jerry Senior were given the task of making a synthetic artery. Von Liebig redirected Meadox to develop woven materials that could be used in the human circulatory system. After closing the larger mill, a small experimental mill was set up in a two-car garage in Haledon, N.J. [2]

The challenge in creating artificial blood vessels is that a single tube must branch into two. The problem is the bifurcation point, which always leaked (the tubular part was not a problem to weave). Jerry Senior was finally able to develop a technique for weaving a bifurcation that did not leak. He succeeded in cutting cards that controlled the looms to make a series of side-by-side bifurcated blood vessels, woven aortas.

As is described in a Juniata College obituary for William von Liebig (a graduate who made a substantial gift to Juniata), "When the Haffa conglomerate began to crumble in 1960, Mr. von Liebig bought the Meadox Weaving Company over lunch in November of 1960 for $25,000. The deal was finalized in January of 1961. He changed the name to Meadox Medicals, Inc." [3] Jerry Senior was asked at the time if he would like to be part of this new venture. Having three children and another on the way, he was concerned that it would be too much risk. They then worked out a deal where Jerry Senior would pay von Liebig one dollar for all the Meadox Mill's card cutting machines and other support equipment. He could then start his own textile business, but at the same time he committed to keeping Meadox Medicals as a client and doing the card cutting and design for them. Jerry Valenta & Sons, Inc. was born.

Jerry Senior's two sons, Jerry and Gene, went to work for the family business as teenagers. Both had to learn the skill of card cutting, which involved hours of practice. Jerry Senior's wife, Helen, an English teacher, supported the new business with letter writing and communication tasks.

Jerry Valenta & Sons grew and developed a reputation for accuracy and workmanship. They worked with many different fabric designers, and they punched the cards that drove the looms to weave a wide variety of fabrics. Jerry learned a great deal about the process of fabric design from the fabric designers and the technicians who serviced the looms. It would serve him well later in his career when Jerry Valenta & Sons acquired a small number of looms and began doing small-run specialty weaving.

In my discussions with Jerry about the history of the business, there were three phases of the business's development:

I. Public Card Cutting

Jerry's father was a master card cutter. Valenta & Sons' business began with two customers: Meadox Medical's vein weaving and Ronitex Jacquard Mills' decorative weaving. With more and more customers, Valenta & Sons hired additional professional card cutters. Among other woven products, they cut the cards for making neckties, bedspreads, and labels. The mills that wove these articles were located in different parts of the country. Jerry Valenta & Sons became the link between the designers and the mills that did the actual weaving.

II. Selling and Supporting Jacquard Weaving Machinery

In 1963 Jerry Senior went to the International Textile Machinery Exposition in Hanover, Germany, where he arranged to become the U.S. sales representative for a group of firms in three fields related to Jacquard weaving: (1) Jacquard looms and card cutting machinery, (2) blank Jacquard cards, lubricants and mill supplies, and (3) Jacquard harnesses, the link between the Jacquard card reader and the loom.

After the International Textile Machinery Exposition, the public card cutting venture morphed into a sales and technical service organization that supplied Jacquard weaving mills. Over the years they sold thousands of looms and ancillary hardware. They also provided service for Grosse looms, which they represented, with technicians who came from Germany on short-term work visas. Ultimately they set up a school in South Carolina to train Grosse-certified mechanics.

specialty products. They later purchased newer looms that utilize digital media to control the weaving process. Gene, who had specialized in sales, became less involved with the business as it moved into specialty production.

There are two ways that looms are given their weaving instructions at Valenta & Sons. The older looms are driven by punches on "Verdol" cards. These are long strips of yellow plasticized paper that have on them the circular punches that control the loom. (You can see these "cards" in many of the photographs of the older looms.) The Verdol system can run a loom much faster than the traditional cardboard Jacquard cards.

The Verdol cards are "punched" by a machine directly from computer instructions created from the fabric design. No card punchers are necessary. Valenta & Sons' two newest looms dispense with even the Verdol cards. They are run directly by the computer instructions that come from the fabric design. In this latest transformation of the business, the card cutting skills with which Jerry Senior started the business are no longer needed.

In the heyday of the sales and support business, Jerry's sister Gale ran the technical, art, and customer service end of the business. Jerry's brother-in-law Walter, having experience in paper manufacturing, ran the supply and harness-building department. Gene was in charge of machinery sales. All these departments worked closely together.

In the mid-60s they began to develop a method for using computers to produce textile fabrics. They created a method to digitize an artist's drawing, and they developed software that used the digitized designs to control a loom. This replaced two trades that were once key parts of Jacquard weaving: converting the designers' work into a grid (which guided the card cutters) and then the actual card cutting. Jerry Valenta & Sons was participating in a major transformation in the textile industry, computer-controlled weaving. Mills began purchasing their own computerized weaving systems, and the vendors who supplied the automated systems often provided the hardware, supplies, and support that Valenta & Sons offered. Over time, the Valentas' service business began to fall off. This led to the third phase of Jerry Valenta & Sons' business.

In the early 1980s, Jerry Senior passed away. He was only 68, which left Jerry and his brother Gene to begin running the business.

III. Short-Run Specialty Production Added to the Mix

With the decline of the sales and service business, Jerry and Gene decided to begin a small weaving operation of their own. They purchased four looms at auction, and began weaving

2018 Perspective

Jerry Valenta & Sons is now run by Jerry (son of the founder) and his son Richard. While each of them performs all the work needed to some extent, Rich runs the business end of things and he is the person who converts the fabric designs into computerized instructions that create Verdol cards or directly run the newest digitally-controlled looms. Jerry is more involved in the hardware than business operations. He prefers to work on loom setup and maintenance, and he still does some technical service work.

Unlike his brother Gene who is now retired, Jerry has no interest in retiring. In addition to the family business, Valenta & Sons has assisted several museums that have exhibits of Jacquard looms and peripheral equipment. Jerry and his brother Gene both collect woven silk "novelties." These novelties include the woven calendars that mills used to give to their customers at Christmas time. Also, they include some much more complex works of art such as a woven silk drawing, a group portrait, of the signers of the Declaration of Independence, woven on a huge loom. Jerry looks forward to having Valenta & Sons weaving some novelties of their own.

• • •

Jerry Valenta & Sons is unique amongst the artisan business in this book in that there are no employees. It is run by a father and son with deep knowledge of weaving, the mechanical aspects of Jacquard looms, and the computerization that now controls the creation of fabric on these looms.

Footnotes:

1. New York Times, August 6, 1954, Meadox Weaving Company notice of sale to Titus Haffa.

2. Journal of Vascular Surgery, Volume 27, No. 1, article accepted June 10, 1997: Robert B. Smith III, MD, "Presidential address, The foundations of modern aortic surgery."

3. Juniata | Campus News Article 188, April 14, 2000: "William J. von Liebig Gift Leads Science Center Drive."

Photographs in Jerry Valenta & Sons Introduction

Page 19: Jerry Valenta "entering the reed"

In the process of weaving, the threads (or "ends") that run from the front of the loom to the back of the loom are called the "warp." In a modern loom, the warp may consist of over 10,000 threads that lay side-by-side across the loom. The more threads in a warp, the wider a piece of fabric can be woven at one time. The "weft," refers to the threads that run perpendicular to the warp. Weft threads are carried across the loom by shuttles, and each successive thread in the weft may be a different color. The Jacquard cards or the digital media that control the weaving can control the color of the weft threads used.

The threads in a new warp are being tied to the threads in the old warp. This is done so the old threads (or "ends") will pull the new ones through the parts of the loom. You may need a new warp because the threads have run out in the old warp or because you are starting a new job on the loom and you need different colors/types of thread for the weaving.

The reed, a device that looks like a long, very fine comb, controls the spacing of the warp ends on the loom, and different jobs may require combs with different spacing. When switching warps, Jerry cuts off the ends of the old warp. In this photograph, Jerry is using a "reed knife" (flat blade with a hook at the end) to pull the threads through the reed. The ends alternate, one higher and the next lower.

Page 21: Two Dornier looms

These are the newest, widest, and fastest looms at Valenta & Sons mill. These looms are driven using magnetic media rather than punched cards.

On the left is a good view of "accumulators." The shuttles that carry the threads in the woof back-and-forth move very fast. You cannot pull the thread off of a cone fast enough without breaking it. The accumulator pulls the yarn off of the cone and holds it loosely so that the shuttle can whip across the loom and pull the yarn smoothly. On these high-speed looms, the accumulators are a part of the loom itself. On older, slower looms, the accumulator may be optional.

Plate 1 *Tying in a new warp. Here, Jerry's son, Rich, is holding the ends in his hand while Jerry uses the reed knife to pull the ends through the reed. Having someone else hand you the next thread can speed up this operation by five or six times.*

Plate 2 *Jerry Valenta leaning on the loom as he threads ends through the reed. Since this is time-consuming and hard on the back, Jerry uses the position seen in the photo to ease back strain.*

Plate 3 *Frank Torresola using a 1940s-vintage knot tying machine. Here, he is working at the back of one of Valenta & Sons' Dornier looms, their newest looms. Torresola is "tying in" a new warp. The Dornier looms can handle a warp with 12,000 threads. Assuming you are not changing the spacing with a different reed, the goal is to tie each of the ends on the new warp to the corresponding thread on the old warp. The loom can then pull the small knots joining old and new ends through the rollers, the drop wires, the heddle, and the reed.*

Tying 12,000 knots in fine (and sometimes slippery) threads is extraordinarily time consuming. Manually, it would take weeks. The process can be sped up considerably using a knot-tying machine.

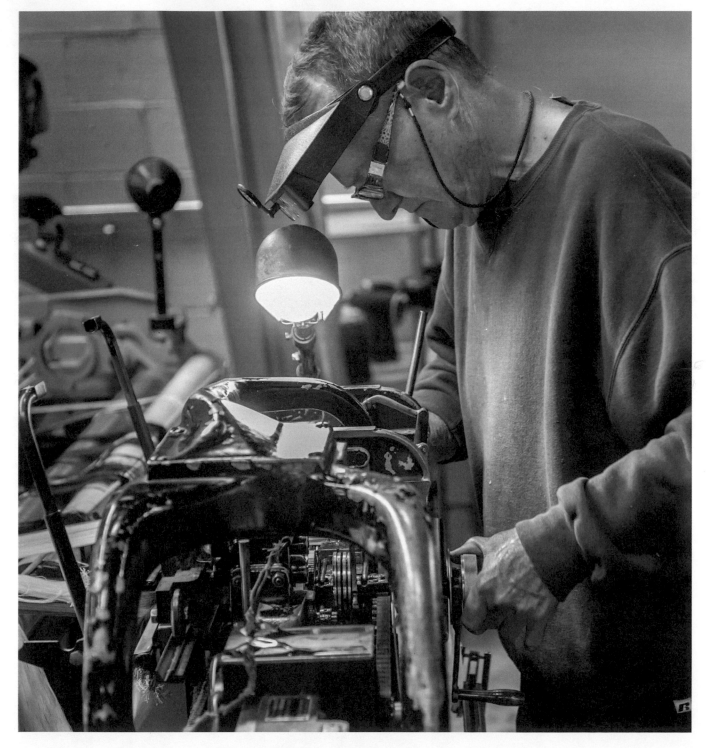

Plate 4 *Hand cranking the knot-tying machine to test whether it is set up properly. When the old and new ends are aligned in the correct order, the machine will move from thread-to-thread and tie a simple overhand knot that joins the ends in the old and new warps. While this machine must be set up multiple times to handle the 12,000 ends in a Dornier loom warp, the whole operation can be accomplished in approximately four hours.*

Plate 5 *Jerry Valenta "Entering the Heddle." The vertical yellow cords are part of the harness that translates the punches on cards to the raising and lowering of threads on the warp as weaving takes place. The cords are tied to metal pieces that have small "eyes" through which the threads pass. (The metal hooks ("reed hooks") are being used to mark the position in the warp on which Jerry is working.)*

Plate 6 *Microswitches. Threads in the woof are fed through these microswitches, which will stop the loom if a thread breaks. Accumulators are not necessary on a slower loom, whereas they are essential to keep the thread from breaking in the high-speed Dornier looms pictured earlier.*

Plate 7 *Guides for the woof threads on one of the older looms.*

Plate 8 *Side view of an older Verdol loom head, a far less elegant design than the later Grosse mechanism (shown in the next plate). The loom head, located above the loom itself, is the machine that reads the punches in the Jacquard cards and converts them into the motions that make the loom function.*

Plate 9 *Side view of the head mechanism for a Grosse loom. (Valenta & Sons sold thousands of Grosse looms, a later version than the one shown here, to textile mills.) Jerry Valenta commented that whenever the mills could, they would try to standardize on a single kind of loom. Maintaining different kinds of looms took substantially more training, and it was not cost-effective.*

Plate 10
*Interior of
loom head
mechanism.*

Plate 11 *Jacquard Still Life I. Shuttles, tools, and Jacquard cards on a loom between jobs.*

Plate 12 *Jacquard Still Life II.*

Plate 13 *Breakage stops (or drop wires) detail. A breakage stop rides along the top of each thread in the warp. If the thread breaks, the breakage stop drops, completes an electrical circuit, which in turn stops the loom immediately.*

Plate 14 *Breakage stop detail II.*

Plate 15 *Loom Harness Study I. The harness is a network of cords that transmit the weaving instructions from the head above to the heddle, the part of the loom that raises or lowers each thread in the warp so the weft thread can pass through and create the woven fabric.. One harness cord is required for each vertical wire in the heddle and the thread that passes through it. This plate, and the following four explore the patterns created by the cords in the loom harness.*

Plate 16 *Loom Harness Study II.*

Plate 17 Loom Harness Study III.

Plate 18 Loom Harness Study IV.

Plate 19 *Loom Harness Study V. Note the glass rods under the Jacquard head. They reduce friction on the harness cords as they move up and down.*

CHAPTER TWO

GREAT FALLS
METALWORKS

During the period December 2014 through April 2015, I made a number of trips to Paterson, New Jersey, to photograph Great Falls Metalworks, a jewelry manufacturer in a former silk mill. Jan Palombo and her husband Michael Brothers started the firm. When I photographed the business, Jan was running it with her daughter Flora Brothers. Michael had passed away in 2007. This history of the firm is based on conversations I had with Jan Palombo in the winter of 2014-15, but the bulk of the information comes from an interview with Jan in April of 2018.

Jan graduated from Tufts University and the Boston Museum School. In her early twenties, she moved to New Orleans where she was a schoolteacher. There she met Michael Brothers, whom she later married. In 1967 they moved to San Francisco, as Jan describes it, "because it was in the air." Michael got a job in Oakland as a welder, building ships. They had no money, and in the beginning, they lived in their car or on the street.

Jan needed to earn some income. One week, she took half of Michael's check, and used the money to purchase a small Butane torch, welding rods, and a roll of muslin, inexpensive fabric used as liner material for mattresses and furniture. With these she produced jackets and shirts in a flowing hippie style that was popular at the time. She made buttons by creating design impressions in sand on the Alameda shore where Michael worked. She melted the brass rods and dripped the metal into the depressions in the sand. These castings became the buttons, belt buckles, and hooks on the shirts and dresses she sold. She found a store, the African Store on Telegraph Road in Berkeley, that sold her clothing.

The owner told her that the sewing was not that good but that people really liked the buttons. So Jan started making jewelry. Jimi Hendrix was a customer of hers, and he ordered huge brass and copper gauntlets.

Thus, Jan started her career as a jewelry maker, and Michael continued working as a welder.

In June of 1968 they moved to Paterson, New Jersey, to be closer to Michael's grandmother who was sick and living there at the time. Jan found a $70 a month railroad apartment. They lived, and she worked, there. Later, as the business expanded, they took over the bottom floor, a former saloon. Jan became pregnant.

They then found a doctor's office on 32nd Street. They turned the various rooms in the doctor's office into their jewelry atelier. Business took off. Jan described people coming to Paterson and standing in line to buy their pieces.

The next move was to buy the factory of an eighty-year-old stained glass maker. At this point, they had 25 employees. As Jan described it, they tried to follow their values in hiring employees.

While working on this project, I restored some old photographs for Jan. There were pictures of gatherings of employees and their families. When we discussed these photos, Jan spoke then about having Vietnamese refugees who worked for them and how they tried to

support their employees' families.

Jan traveled to purchase rough stone for the jewelry, and she needed to find stonecutters. With two Chinese-speaking friends, she went to Hong Kong. They found an ad from a stonecutter who was offering to cut stones and who had a history of cutting malachite. She eventually found the stonecutter. They could not communicate until they met a local woman, who spoke a little English, translated for them, and told their fortunes – assuring them both that the other was highly trustworthy. Jan paid the stonecutter $6,000 in cash which he used to start up a stone-cutting factory for her in Hong Kong and later in Shenzhen. The factory still exists; the stonecutter was,

Michael Brothers, third from left, and crew pouring floors at mill on 22nd Street in Paterson. (restored from Kodachrome print provided by J. Palombo.)

indeed, very reliable. Jan would purchase uncut stones, ship them in containers to the factory, and the stonecutter would return ship small packages of the polished, custom cut stones to Great Falls Metalworks.

Jan showed me examples of inlaid stonework that she designed and which the Chinese factory executed. She did not want to waste the little pieces of stone left over from the cutting operations. She thought of quilts and how the pieces of stone could fit together to form complicated inlaid designs used in many varieties of cufflinks, for example.

On April 24, 1986 (Jan's birthday), Michael took her to see an abandoned 1920s silk mill in Paterson: 301 East 22nd Street. He had made a bid on the building, and this became their factory until around 2015. The building required a huge amount of work. Michael and their employees would work at their operating location until late afternoon and then go to the 22nd Street building and work until late in the evening. They built all the missing windows, rebuilt the floors and roof, poured concrete on the first floor, and fixed all the systems in the building.

During the height of the business (from 1978 to 2000) the firm had a total revenue of around $45 million. Jan did all the designing and ran the business. She had employees who did billing, shipping, and accounting. She went to China twice a year to meet with the man who ran the lapidary. When Caroline Kennedy was married in 1986, her mother Jackie Kennedy bought all the bridesmaids' bracelets from Great Falls Metalworks.

Michael was a brilliant machinist. On the ground floor of the silk mill, he created a workshop in which he produced jigs, dies, and special tools, which made possible more efficient jewelry manufacturing. Photographs of this machine shop are included in the photo series about Great Falls Metalworks.

The business was beginning to decline after 2000, but Jan sees the 2008 recession as the real downturn for the business. In 2007 both Jan and Michael had cancer, and Michael passed away. At that time, they still had 12 to 15 employees.

There were many changes taking place: in 2000, Great Falls Metalworks had roughly 5,000 active customers (catalogs, museum shops, department stores, etc.); by 2007 the number was down to 2,400. The company had boutiques in Bloomingdales, Bambergers, and Saks. In many cases, their jewelry was competing against far less expensive pieces from Asia.

Jan also talked about changing tastes at the time. Young people used to like jewelry; they began to prefer tattoos and electronics. Economic forces and changing taste were the main forces behind Great Falls Metalworks' decline.

By the mid-teens, the building was in disrepair, with a leaking roof and heating problems. (See the photographs of workers bundled up in heavy coats making jewelry.) Jan's daughter, Flora, was increasingly involved in the business. Besides Jan and Flora, at the time, there were three employees making jewelry and two doing office work and shipping.

As of 2018, the building on 22nd Street in Paterson had been sold. Flora continues to run a very scaled-down version of the business from a different location.

I asked Jan about the conflict between art and commerce. She considered herself an artist, but for her, the real issue was being a woman. She was never treated as the person who ran the business. She was treated as her husband's secretary. Michael would have to sign for loans and contracts, and she would co-sign. Nevertheless, she found ways to cope with these issues. As Jan described it, if you are successful, it is easy to find business people to work for you. This allowed her to focus on jewelry design.

Jan now considers herself to be completely out of the business. My photographs represent Great Falls Metalworks at the end of its life in Paterson, New Jersey. This is the story of a business that began as one woman's passion, became a multi-million dollar manufacturing operation, and has now become a much smaller operation run by the founder's daughter.

Jan summed up the history of Great Falls Metalworks: "It was of its time. The delight in artisan work. Rage against the machine. That moment has passed."

Plate 20 *Jan Palombo, the founder of the business, setting a stone in an earring.*

Plate 21 *A rubber injection mold. The mold is created from a model of the piece of jewelry being made. Great Falls used the services of skilled mold cutters to prepare molds that align properly and separate easily. The mold contains a sprue, which is a channel that allows heated wax to flow into the cavity in the mold. The wax replica of the model is turned into the piece of metal jewelry using the "lost wax" casting method: The wax replica from the mold is placed in a cylinder and surrounded with "plaster investment," a plaster-of-Paris-like material that resists heat. After the plaster investment dries, it is heated to a high temperature, the wax melts out of the cylinder, and silver or gold is poured into the void left by the wax. The plaster investment is broken away, and the resulting precious metal piece becomes the jewelry – a replica of the original model.*

Plate 22 *Polishing a ring.*

Plate 23 *Sorting Peruvian opal briolettes. The briolette cut is a pear-shaped stone with facets. The stones must be must be sorted into matched pairs for earrings.*

Plate 24 *Tapping a ring to harden the metal. Because of problems with the heating system in the refurbished silk mill, employees wore winter coats at their work benches.*

Plate 25 *Drilling out a bead using a diamond drill.*

Plate 26 *Using an oxy-acetylene torch to solder jump rings for use on a pendant. A jump ring is a metal ring (usually circular) that can be used to hold together the components of a piece of jewelry.*

Plate 27 *Soldering a jump ring together using an oxy-acetylene torch.*

54

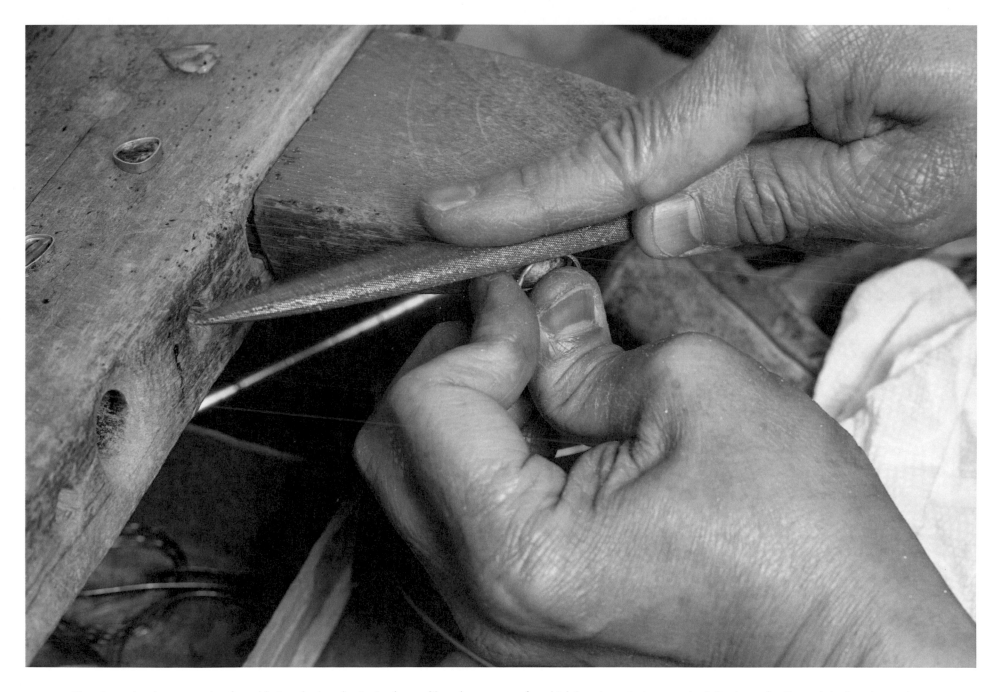

Plate 28 *Cleaning a ring in preparation for soldering the bezel to it. On the workbench are stones for which bezels are being matched. Opals are fragile, and the bezel must be the right size and shape to hold the stone securely and not damage it.*

Plate 29
Soldering 28-gauge silver wire for earrings. This must be done very quickly so that the silver wire does not melt and the stone, already attached to the earring, is not damaged.

Plate 30 *Measuring bracelets. These bracelets have been created from cast sterling silver horses.*

Plate 31 *Flora Brothers, Jan Palombo's daughter, now runs Great Falls Jewelry. Here she is setting a stone using a ring mandrel to hold the ring in position. The ring mandrel, a jeweler's tool used to measure the size of rings, is a steel rod that tapers toward the end and has ring sizes marked on the steel shaft. The mandrel in this photograph does not have sizes marked; rather, it is used to hold a ring while working on it.*

Plate 32 *Plastic drawers of beads used as accents in pieces of jewelry.*

Plate 33 *Cabinets containing a small part of the huge inventory of gemstones used by Great Falls to manufacture jewelry.*

Plate 34 *A collection of clamps and jigs on a shelf in Michael Brothers' workshop. While Michael Brothers did not himself make jewelry, he created a wide variety of tools and jigs that facilitated more efficient jewelry production.*

Plate 35 *An abandoned time clock in Michael Brothers' workshop, an artifact from the period when Great Falls Metalworks had a much larger work force.*

Plate 36 *A collection of dies in Michael Brothers' workshop. These dies, made from tool steel, are part of a group of dies purchased in Providence, Rhode Island. The designs on the faces of these dies were sometimes incorporated as artistic elements in objects created for museum gift shops.*

Plate 37 *[left] Setting an opal inlay into a cufflink. The bezel around the inlay must be tapped gently to hold the stone inlay without damaging it. The metal block on which the cufflink is being hammered is a jig created by Michael Brothers to help position cufflinks as they are being assembled.*

Plate 38 *Making jump rings using a needle nose pliers.*

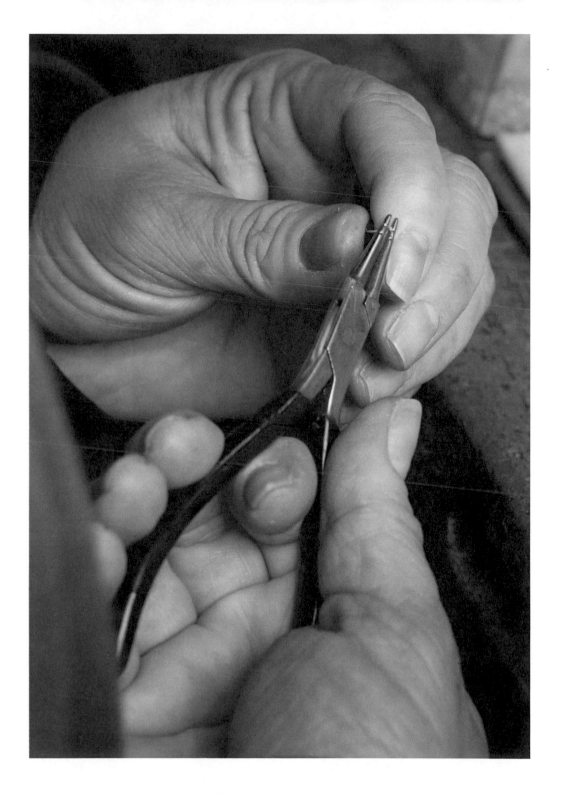

Plate 39 *Sorting faceted beads into pairs for earrings.*

Plate 40 *Hammering a ring.*

Plate 41 *[left]*
Applying red rouge (a compound of iron oxide and wax) to a polishing rod. The rod is made of wood covered with felt, and it is used for polishing the inside of rings.

Plate 42
Polishing a cufflink. This is the second to last step in which a compound called "white diamond" (zinc and wax) is used on the buffing wheel.

Chapter Three

Peragallo Pipe Organ Company

The Peragallo Pipe Organ Company is a family-owned business now in its fourth generation.

The business was founded by John Peragallo Sr. in 1918. By the time he started his own business at the age of 22, he had already had a wide range of experience in the world of organ building.

John Sr. came to America at the age of three. His parents brought their family from Italy in 1898. They started an Italian restaurant on 54th Street and 2nd Avenue in New York City, and in his earliest years, John Sr. helped with the family business. He wanted to do more:

> By the time [John Sr.] was 12 he was anxious to get started on a career of his own. At the same time Ernest M. Skinner was gaining great acclaim for the fine organs he was building. When cathedrals and churches in New York City wanted the very best of everything, the organ was an E. M. Skinner. John Peragallo joined Skinner's maintenance crew that worked under the distinguished guidance of Fred L. Wilck. John learned fast, and he was soon tuning and regulating reeds in addition to his other maintenance chores. After five years of this excellent training under a master craftsman, he was ready for something bigger. Fred Wilck hated to lose John and regretted that the Skinner Company couldn't offer John a higher-paying job. However, he didn't wish to hold him back, and therefore he encouraged John to move to a new organ company that was being formed in the booming industrial city of Paterson, New Jersey.[1]

While the E. M. Skinner Company built pipe organs primarily for churches, the firm John Peragallo Sr. joined in Paterson, New Jersey, built more organs for motion picture theaters than for churches.

> Paterson, which is just west of New York City, had a reputation for aggressively attracting new industries. The president of Paterson's Chamber of Commerce was James T. Jordan, who was very successful in the piano manufacturing business. In 1915 he encouraged three enterprising young musicians to form a company to build organs… They decided to call the company the "American Master Organ Company."
>
> John Peragallo, stepped into this [new firm] as head of the electrical wiring department.
>
> During the first two years of operation the company turned out five theater organs … and four church organs. The theater organs had "piano consoles." The

top manual was a piano keyboard, and the pipes were [in most cases] located in cabinets in the orchestra pit.

…one day there was great excitement around the American Master Organ Company. Frank White had bid on a deal with the Silver Bar Amusement Company of Butte, Montana, that would set a new standard for organbuilding excellence. It was to be a 30-rank organ with four manuals. Wurlitzer's quote was $45,000, and the American Master quote was $20,000. [2]

The Butte, Montana, theater organ was to be American Master Organ Company's greatest accomplishment and its downfall.

After eight months of work in the factory, the organ was almost ready to ship to Butte. The Tuba and Diapasons had arrived from Samuel Piece's pipe shop in Massachusetts. Most of the organ had been assembled and tested in the erecting room in Paterson. …the vacuum-operated percussions had caused problems from the beginning, and they still were not working properly. However the theater was ready for the organ, and the installation had to get started or the American Master Organ Company would be liable for a $100 per day penalty that was part of the contract. In March, 1917, the organ left Paterson for the long trip by rail to Butte, Montana. The percussions were to be shipped later.

A few days later on March 20, John Peragallo boarded the Nickelplate RR line to begin almost four months of frustration as the installation foreman. [2]

They were unable to get the organ ready to play on opening night.

…in fact an orchestra played the pictures for several weeks while the organ was being finished. At last it was ready to try…. The organ sounded magnificent. Everyone was very pleased. The acoustics of the theater, coupled with the fine pipework and voicing, produced a sound that was unforgettable. In fact, the volume of the 32' Diaphones had to be reduced because the beautiful glass partitions at the rear of the theater shattered from the vibration. The result lived up to the motto of the American Master Organ Company: "Science, Musicianship, Craft; Master Workmen to Master Musician." [2]

They completed the instrument. However, disaster followed:

The Butte organ and poor management had bankrupted the firm. They wired John Peragallo $71.80 to cover his fare, and told him to come home; they were bankrupt. So on July 16, 1917, he left Butte--never to return.

When [John Peragallo Sr.] arrived in Paterson, he found that the previously thriving little company had disintegrated…. [James T.] Jordan [who had founded the company] encouraged Peragallo to remain in Paterson and continue in the organ business. Peragallo acquired the logo with the motto and some of the shop machinery from the American Master Organ Company and founded his own company, the Peragallo Organ Company, in 1918. [2]

At the age of 22, John Peragallo Sr. was the owner of his own pipe organ company.

The Peragallo Company's history continues the story:

The early years of the Peragallo Organ Company introduced John Sr. to some lifelong friends who moved the company through its first decades. Monsignor Carlo Cianci, an Italian American pastor and community leader, commissioned John's first new organ at St. Michael's Church in Paterson, New Jersey. In his travels back to service organs in New York and see his family, John was introduced to Octavia Rolandelli… Octavia was a wonderful concert pianist in her own right and held a degree from the Manhattan School of Business. They were wed in the fall of 1925 and formed a perfect partnership as she managed the administrative end of the business while John ran the organ shop.

The first new organ John installed at St. Michael's reflects many of the E.M. Skinner tonal ideas and detailed engineering he had learned in his youth. His good friend and fellow Italian, Pietro Yon, dedicated this first work while expanding his celebrated career at St. Patrick's Cathedral on 5th Avenue in New York City. [3]

Several factors have contributed to the firm's long-term success. This is a family business and one that successfully involved each of the next three succeeding generations. The tonal design of their instruments followed John Sr.'s experience at the E. M. Skinner Company. Peragallo has not been afraid to utilize complex electrical, pneumatic, and later electronic technologies in their instruments. The technology may have been "bleeding edge" in the Butte, Montana, theater organ, but the Peragallos have used technology with care to provide wide capabilities coupled with reliability.

The final factor leading to long-term success is the close ties that Peragallo Organ Company forged with Catholic clergy and musicians. While Peragallo certainly builds instruments for churches of other denominations, their connection to Catholic clergy and musicians is an important reason why the Peragallo Organ Company continues to thrive after one hundred years.

In 1949 John Peragallo Jr. joined his father in the business. His obituary in the New York Times provides a short history of his life and work:

> John Stephen Peragallo Jr. was born on Feb. 11, 1932, in Manhattan and grew up in Paterson. His father, John Sr., had been an apprentice to the renowned organ builder Ernest M. Skinner before starting his own company. John Jr. studied at the Newark College of Engineering before joining his father's business in 1949. For years, father and son lived two houses apart, with the factory in between....

> Mr. Peragallo considered his crowning achievement to be the restoration of the organ at St. Patrick's, a four-year undertaking. The organ had been built by a St. Louis company from 1928 to 1930; more than six decades later, it was in deep need of repair.

> Starting in 1994, Mr. Peragallo and his associates plucked out St. Patrick's pipes in batches and carted them back to Paterson for cleaning. The organ has so many pipes – more than 9,000 – that listeners were never the wiser. Leather valves were replaced, about four dozen bellows were refurbished, the electrical system was upgraded and much else.

> From that year on, Mr. Peragallo's company has provided St. Patrick's with weekly maintenance and, for special occasions, an on-site troubleshooter. For Mr. Peragallo, one particular occasion stood out. On Oct. 7, 1995, Pope John Paul II led prayers at St. Patrick's while visiting New York.

> Mr. Peragallo was there too, perched high in the pipes under the gallery's rose window, nervous as a cat but ready for anything.[4]

John Peragallo Jr. passed away on September 12, 2008. He was succeeded in the business by his sons John III and Frank. John Peragallo III followed in his father's footsteps combining an engineering background with skill as an organist.

> The eldest son, John Peragallo III, had a strong curiosity and natural musical ability from an early age. Soon he was performing the great organ works and landed his first church job as Organist for St. Andrew's Catholic Church in Clifton, New Jersey when he was but 13 years of age. John III continued his studies with … teachers Russell Hayton of Montclair State College and Leonard Raver of the Manhattan School of Music in New York City. His organ studies also brought him to France to play the historic instruments of Europe. John III's academic studies at New Jersey Institute of Technology carried the company to the cutting edge of the budding digital technologies of the early '70s, further evolving the way organs were being built and used within church architectures.

> Frank Peragallo, too, was involved from an early age, studying cabinet making with the German cabinet makers on his father's staff. Frank took a keen interest in studying the Canadian and American master organ cabinets and pushed his father to consider the benefits of building in this style. John Jr. allowed his young son to develop the architectural department of the company which began experimenting with chest layouts, caseworks, and carvings.[5]

In 2016 and 2017, when the photographs in this chapter were taken, the firm was run by John III and Frank Peragallo. The next generation is being groomed to run the business. John IV received a Masters Degree in Architecture from Catholic University of America, and Tony Peragallo, Frank's son, received a Master's in Business Finance from Montclair State University. As the company history describes them: "Since his youth Anthony has studied to become a talented voicer, most recently receiving praise from Daniel Roth for his work at St. Francis Xavier. John IV, alongside Frank has pushed the designs and fabrication techniques to develop complex designs and appropriately integrate caseworks into their environments and worked to promote the instrument and its role within the church and musical community."

In more recent years, the firm has greatly expanded its ability to create organ cases in a wide variety of styles. The two photographs at the end of this introduction, Opus 1 in St. Michael Catholic Church in Paterson, NJ, and one of their most recent major installations, the organ for Saints Simon and Jude Cathedral in Phoenix, Arizona, built in 2016, contrast their early and most recent casework.

With each succeeding generation, Peragallo Organ Company has built on its strengths. They continue their E. M. Skinner heritage, though in recent years they have begun incorporating French orchestral organ voicing in some instruments, following in the footsteps of the 19th Century French organ builder Aristide Cavaillé-Coll. Peragallo continues to use technology to enhance their instruments. And their relationships with Catholic musicians and clergy remain strong.

The next generation of the Peragallo Organ Company will not be led by a family member with both engineering expertise and training as a church organist. Of course, John Peragallo Sr. did not have either of these skills. It will be fascinating to see how this family business adapts.

Peragallo Opus 1, Paterson, NJ (photo from Peragallo website)

Footnotes:

1. "THE AMERICAN MASTER ORGAN COMPANY LIVES ON" by John Peragallo as told to Dave Schutt in 1974. This history of The American Master Organ Company was posted on the University of Iowa PIPEORG-L listserv by Dave Schutt, 13 April 1998, https://list.uiowa.edu/scripts/wa.exe?A2=ind9804B&L=PIPORG-L&P=R11328&1=PIPORG-L&9=A&I=-3&J=on&d=No+Match%3BMatch%3BMatches&z=4

2. PIPEORG-L listserv, Dave Schutt, 13 April 1998.

3. From "History of the Peragallo Organ Company" a document supplied by John Peragallo IV in 2018. The basic history of the firm in this introduction comes from that document unless otherwise noted. pp 1-2.

4. "John Peragallo Jr., Who Kept Organs on Key, Dies at 76", obituary in the New York Times, by Margalit Fox, September 22, 2008.

5. "History of the Peragallo Organ Company", page 2.

Peragallo instrument, Saints Simon and Jude, Phoenix, AZ, 2016 (photo from Peragallo website)

Plate 43 *Frank Peragallo designs the casework for the company's instruments. But he is also a skilled woodworker. Here he does the initial cutting on an organ case component.*

Plate 44 *While the Peragallos make extensive use of power tools, work by hand is extremely important in creating their instruments. Here, a piece from an organ console is being sanded.*

Plate 45 *Checking lumber for straightness.*

78

Plate 46 *Setting the expression shoe bar in a console under construction. This is the wooden frame for the console of the organ being built for the Cathedral of Saints Simon and Jude in Phoenix, Arizona.*

Plate 47 *Quality control is integral to building reliable pipe organs. Here, Anthony Peragallo is notating the burn marks on the top of a wind chest to insure that the counter-sinking is correct. Pipes sit in the depressions on the top of the wind chest.*

Plate 48 *Clamping the wood pieces for a console music rack. This is a much later stage in the construction of the Saints Simon and Jude instrument console.*

Plate 49 *The organ is first assembled in the Peragallo shop's erecting room. Pipes on the organ's façade are sometimes decorative; however, here they are speaking pipes that sit atop narrow wind chests that must be supplied with pressurized air that will allow the pipes to sound. Here, Anthony Peragallo is lining up the wind line for a façade chest.*

Plate 50 *Installing wind lines in the organ case. The wind line being installed here supplies air to the façade chest at the top of the photograph.*

Plate 51 *[left] Staining case work in the wood finishing shop. Wood finishing is a critical, if sometimes messy, component in organ building.*

Plate 52 *Peragallo pipe organs utilize electrical circuits to transmit a key press on the console to opening a valve that allows air into the base of an organ pipe. Here, a console is being wired.*

Plate 53 *[left] Wiring the valve-opening mechanism. Beneath each pipe in the wind chest is a solenoid, which, when energized, opens the valve to allow wind to flow into the pipe.*

Plate 54 *Rewiring the pipe valve circuits on a restored wind chest.*

Plate 55 *[left] Wiring the switching circuits inside the organ case. Which pipe or pipes sound is a function both of the keys that are pressed on the organ console and which stops the organist has chosen. A stop is a rank of pipes, with a common sound quality, one for each pitch in the musical scale. There is a great deal of switching circuitry inside a large organ to control which pipes will speak.*

Plate 56 *Emerging from the case of the Saints Simon and Jude instrument after a session of switching circuit wiring.*

Plate 57 *[left] Raising a façade pipe into place.*

Plate 58 *[above] John Peragallo IV checking the plans as he installs a tremolo motor on the wind reservoir.*

Plate 59 *Beginning the installation of one of the chancel organ cases at St. John the Baptist Cathedral in Paterson, NJ.*

Plate 60 *Installing the corbel under the south case of the St. John the Baptist chancel organ.*

Plate 61 *Anthony Peragallo tuning a mixture. A mixture is an organ stop that utilizes multiple ranks of pipe to add brightness and clarity to the overall mix of sound.*

Plate 62 *Voicing: John Peragallo III at the console and Anthony Peragallo at the pipes. The instrument at St. Stephen's Episcopal Church in Armonk, New York, is a 1969 Casavant that was extensively rebuilt and enhanced by the Peragallo Company in 2016.*

Chapter Four

Hiemer Stained Glass Studio

The story of the Hiemer Stained Glass Studio began in Germany and over the decades crisscrossed the globe to its current location in Clifton, New Jersey. Judith and James Van Wie are the owners of Hiemer Stained Glass Studio, with Judith Hiemer Van Wie being the fourth generation of her family creating stained glass windows. Hiemer & Company was founded in Ohio in 1931 by Judi Van Wie's grandfather. Her great-grandfather, who was the first stained glass artisan in the family, later came to the States and joined his son in the new business.

Judi describes her father Gerhard (Gerry), now retired, as a great storyteller with a sense of humor. He wrote a short history of the business: "The Story of Hiemer & Company or How The Geese Almost Ate My Grandfather." The story begins with:

> … Georg Hiemer born 1865 to a farming family in Munich, Bavaria.
>
> From his earliest days [Georg] displayed an extreme distaste for farm chores and a preference for matters artistic. Probably by careful calculation, he proved totally inept at the tasks assigned him as a youth on the farm. At one point, he was assigned to what was ordinarily a girl's chore of minding the flock of geese. That was fine by him because he could sit and draw from nature. However, he even failed at that job because the geese knocked him over and were attempting to consume him when he was rescued by an older, and understanding sister.
>
> At an early age he was paid off by his family, a form of disinheritance, and sent packing.[1]

Georg, who went on to train in art and music, eventually headed the design and painting departments of stained

The sketching process. This is the conceptual stage in which initial drawings are made. The client will review these drawings, which will be re-worked to incorporate changes the client desires. Books, past work of the studio, illustrations of costumes of different periods, and Church history are all sources of input.

glass studios in Germany and Switzerland. He married at the age of thirty and had one son, Edward. Father and son both survived service in the First World War. After the war, both worked for the Munich stained glass studio Von Gerichten.

The Munich Von Gerichten stained glass studio was actually a branch of a US firm with headquarters in Columbus, Ohio. It had been started by a German émigré who had apprenticed at a stained glass studio in Cincinnati, Ohio. He then went on to start his own business, enlisting the services of his older brother. By 1893 the Von Gerichten brothers had relocated to Columbus, Ohio, and had changed the name of the business to the Von Gerichten Art Glass Company. [2]

After the First World War, the American Von Gerichten brothers opened their studio in Munich, Germany, where Judi's great-grandfather and grandfather worked.

While Judi's great-grandfather stayed with the Von Gerichten's Munich studio for a number of years, her grandfather Edward moved on. Around 1920, he journeyed to the Philippines and then to Japan and Mexico City in search of work as a stained glass craftsman. His journey ended in Columbus, Ohio, at the home studio of Von Gerichten Art Glass Company. His father was by then the Director of Art at Von Gerichten's Munich branch. In time, Edward became the head of the design and sales departments in Columbus.

In June of 1927 Edward married. He encouraged his parents to come to the US, and in 1929 they emigrated from Munich to the US. This spared them the political turmoil in Germany in the 1930s; furthermore, it later provided Judi's great-grandfather with employment.

Gerry Hiemer continues the story:

> The Von Gerichten firms failed due to the Depression. Bishop Hartley of Columbus urged Edward to form a studio in order to complete work in progress for the diocese. On April 1, 1931, the firm of Edward W. Hiemer and Company was formed…
>
> Since the only work to be had came from the eastern states and since the few churches being built in Ohio preferred to buy their windows from New York, after finishing the last of the windows then under contract, Hiemer & Company decided to move East. Paterson, New Jersey was selected because of its proximity to New York without the disadvantages of a big city. [3]

In 1932, Judi's father, Gerry, the first child of Edward and Elsie Hiemer was born.

Hiemer & Company survived the Depression and the materials shortages caused by World War II. After the war, with significant increase in business, the craftsmen and artists at the company returned.

For a period after the Second World War, the first three generations of the family worked alongside each other:

> Edward did much planning, blueprinting and model building and Gerhard, by this time, was devoting a lot of after school time to the studio… Georg Hiemer… was working on the full size drawings for windows in Assumption Church in Elizabeth, NJ and the windows for St. Michael Church in Cranford, all of which were in various stages of completion… Georg Hiemer died in 1955, but left [an] incredible legacy; thousands of stained glass windows designed for Churches throughout the world. [4]

After serving in the Korean War, Gerry rejoined the family business. He then went to Europe to study medieval and contemporary stained glass installations. Upon his return, he became more and more active in the management of the business. Edward Hiemer passed away in 1969. Gerry then became president of Hiemer & Company.

Beginning in 1985, Gerry's eldest daughter Judith became a full time member of the firm. In addition to training in fine arts, she completed the apprenticeship program as a stained glass journeyman. She became president of the firm in 1997.

In 1993 Judi married James Van Wie, whom she had met in the Business Administration program at Bryant College.

> James was involved in information technologies with AT&T taking the long commute from Clifton to Somerset each day. This proved to be particularly taxing when their first child was born in 2000.
>
> In order to be able to spend more time with his family, James approached Gerry about coming into the family business. Gerry was at an age where retirement looked extremely inviting but he was reluctant to leave Judi running the firm with a new baby in tow. His immediate response, and he did not miss a heartbeat, was, "I'm out, you're in!" Judith and James have been running the studio together since then with Judi focusing on the new stained glass projects and James managing the restorations which have become a major part of the studio's production in recent years. [5]

The Hiemer Stained Glass Studio has embraced modern technology. The business is managed using computers. And yet, making stained glass windows has changed little from the way the craft was carried out in the Middle Ages. As you look at the photographs in this section, most of the work is still done using hand tools. However, soldering irons are now electric, as are drills with wire brushes that are used to clean and remove oxidation from the solder joints in old stained glass windows.

THE APPRENTICESHIP PROGRAM: JOURNEYMAN IN STAINED GLASS

Hiemer Stained Glass is committed to insuring that this ancient craft continues. Training today to become a stained glass artisan is carried out in a manner similar to that in the Middle Ages.

During his career, Gerry was influential in the promotion of Apprentice Training in New Jersey. He worked with the Stained Glass Association of America to revise its apprenticeship and training standards to reflect the nature of the craft in the late 20th century. Those are the standards apprentices today adhere to, completing hours of work experience in various aspects of the trade. It is the same method of training used in medieval times by trade guilds to develop a highly skilled work force.

After establishing the new standards, Hiemer set forth to have the program certified by both the Federal and State Departments of Labor. Both levels of government recognize the Clifton studio as an apprenticeship-training center for stained glass craft. The studio most recently graduated Nutley, New Jersey resident Linda Ebertz who fulfilled the 6,000-hour on the job experience and the 432-hour related schoolwork requirements. The studio currently has three other Journeymen on staff including Gerry's oldest daughter, Judith. [6]

Soldering meeting joints on a new stained glass panel.

The Journeyman program is not like an academic program. Apprenticeships are project-driven. If a firm needs additional help, it will hire an individual who may be given the option to become an apprentice. The 6,000 hours of work experience encompass different aspects of stained glass making. If an apprentice does not get the hours of training/experience in all the required areas, she or he will need additional work to get that experience. The apprenticeship period is typically 3-5 years, but it can last longer. [7]

BUSINESS CYCLES IN STAINED GLASS

The depression and WW II were difficult periods for the firm.

There was a period around the 1970s when, as Judi described it, the Catholic Church became more ecumenical, resulting in less concern about church decoration and stained glass windows. This caused business to slow in the 1970s and 1980s. During that time

Gerry Hiemer's wife Josephine (Judi's mother) ran a gift shop at the studio location. By the 1990s, the firm's traditional business was picking up again.

Interestingly, in the southern states, with more growth in Catholic parishes, there is now more stained glass work in the South than in the North.

STYLES IN STAINED GLASS WINDOWS

In Gerry Hiemer's story of the business, he addresses the different artistic styles in which they have worked:

…the emphasis had always been on ecclesiastical stained glass, specializing in the iconography for Catholic Churches. In 1931 Romanesque and Gothic revival was in vogue. This trend was the mainstay of the studio until the end of World War II when the inspiration for more contemporary design seems to have come from Europe. There was constant competition with European studios exporting to the United States so it was important for the studio to keep up with artistic changes… [8]

Some churches still want traditional stained glass, but making stained glass windows for an entire church is every expensive, not "cost-effective" as Judi put it. Where they see traditional work is when a church with traditional windows wants to add one or two more and they need to match the style of the older windows. Hiemer is happy to oblige.

Judi commented that convents are the places where they are doing some of their most innovative and exciting work. The sisters are much more willing to embrace new styles and techniques than are the parish churches.

•　　　　•　　　　•

The Hiemer Stained Glass Studio is a small organization with a fascinating blend of art and commerce. And the fact that four of the key employees as well as Judi Hiemer Van Wie, her father, grandfather, and great-grandfather were all Stained Glass Journeymen, provides a sense of cohesion and direction that pervades the firm's work.

Footnotes:

1. Manuscript of "The Story of Hiemer & Company or How The Geese Almost Ate My Grandfather." By Gerhard Hiemer, provided by Judith Van Wie, page 1 Gerhard Hiemer prepared this manuscript for a speech he gave at the Stained Glass Association of America conference in Toronto in 1985.

2. From the entry "Von Gerichten Art Glass Company", Rogers Park/West Ridge Historical Society, HistoryWiki, https://www.rpwrhs.org/w/index.php?title=Von_Gerichten_Art_Glass_Company (link as of 2018-11-17).

3. Hiemer, "The Story of Hiemer & Company or How The Geese Almost Ate My Grandfather," page 3.

4. Hiemer, "The Story of Hiemer & Company or How The Geese Almost Ate My Grandfather," page 4.

5. From a research document provided by Judith Van Wie: "Hiemer & Company Stained Glass Studio," The document was prepared by Joe Hawrylko for an article about Hiemer Stained Glass Studio in the January 2012 issue of "Clifton Merchant Magazine," Volume 17, Issue 1, January 6, 2012.

6. Clifton Merchant Magazine, "Hiemer & Company Stained Glass Studio."

7. Notes from a conversation with Judith Hiemer Van Wie, October 29, 2018.

8. Hiemer, "The Story of Hiemer & Company or How The Geese Almost Ate My Grandfather," page 5.

Plate 63 *Inking a sketch for a stained glass window. After approval of the drawing, this is the second step in converting the drawing into a stained glass window. (The first step is making the pencil sketch.)*

Plate 64 *Judith Hiemer Van Wie is the fourth generation of the Hiemer family that has been creating stained glass windows. Here she is researching a stained glass window design. There are many sources that go into the window concept.*

Plate 65 *Creating a full-size "cartoon." This cartoon is based on the inked drawing shown in Plate 63. The inked drawing is copied to acetate and then the image is projected onto a full size piece of paper. The cartoon becomes the basis of the pattern pieces used to cut each of the component pieces of stained glass in the panel.*

Plate 66 *Matting stained glass pieces on the light box. Drawing on pieces of stained glass is done using "matt" – here a mixture of black pigment mixed with ground glass. The matt is applied to the glass and then the details of the drawing are created by thinning or removing the matt using small brushes. The remaining matt is baked onto the glass. Because the matt is glass-based, it becomes a permanent part of the stained glass panel.*

Plate 67 *Touching up hair coloring. Hair tone is applied to the back side of this figure using a small brush. The hair color is created using a pigment that is mixed with ground glass and baked to make it permanent.*

Plate 68 *Consulting on a restoration job. Measurements are critical. Re-framing may require the dimensions of the stained glass to be changed subtly.*

Plate 69 *Re-installing restored stained glass windows at Sacred Heart Church in Clifton, NJ.*

Plate 70 *Using grozing pliers to clean up the edges of a piece of stained glass. The glass was cut from a larger piece by scoring it with a diamond wheel glass cutter and snapping the glass on the scored line. With stained glass, little flakes of glass often remain on the scoring line. These are cleaned off with grozing pliers.*

Plate 71 *In a window restoration, cleaning old glazing compound out of a lead channel.*

Plate 72 *Preparing the panel to be soldered.*

Plate 73 *Using a glazing knife to cut off an old piece of lead came. Lead came is strips of lead, often "H" shaped in cross section, that are used to frame the individual pieces of stained glass and hold them in position in the design. In restoration work, the lead came is reused when possible, but it can be so damaged it must be replaced.*

Plate 74
Soldering broken lead joints on a window restoration. The bowing of the glass in an old stained glass window often causes the lead joints to crack.

Plate 75 *Cleaning glass in preparation for cutting. The wheel of the diamond cutter glides more smoothly over clean glass. Because there are variations in texture and opacity in sheets of stained glass, having clean glass makes it easier to find the best place to cut out a segment of the stained glass window.*

Plate 76 *Creating a full-size drawing for a new stained glass window. The individual pieces of glass in the window are then marked on the drawing, and the marked-up drawing is used to create paper patterns – one for each piece of stained glass to be cut. Here, a pattern is used to score the cut lines for one of the elements in the window.*

Plate 77 *Holding the stained glass up to the light to select the best area for cutting out a piece of a window design.*

Plate 78 *Using a brush drill bit in an electric drill to clean up old solder joints. This is necessary in restorations because the old solder may be covered with a variety of chemicals that make it hard for new solder to adhere. This can be from environmental chemicals on the outsides of stained glass windows as well as bees wax from candles burned inside the church.*

Plate 79 *Checking the dimensions of a panel. The restoration process may cause the panel to enlarge slightly. Sometimes, a new method of framing the window may require a slightly different size. These changes must be taken into account during restoration.*

Plate 80 *Applying glazing compound. After the compound is spread on the window, it is forced into the lead came to make a seal with the glass. This is a critical step in creating a stained glass window that will last.*

Plate 81 *Pressing down the lead came against the glazing compound.*

Plate 82 *Inspecting a finished piece. If any soldered joints are too shiny, lamp black will be used to dull them. After this inspection, the panel is ready to be installed.*

Plate 83 *Measuring a panel to determine the location of support bars. Stained glass windows usually have round support bars running horizontally every 12" to 18". Because of the size of this window, flat vertical support bars were added.*

Plate 84 *The lead came is gently tapped so the joints, where pieces of came meet, will be flat, and the Journeyman can put on a smooth bead of solder.*

CPSIA information can be obtained
at www.ICGtesting.com
Printed in the USA
LVRC100036021221
705066LV00010B/438